Do You Like Butter?

A Poetry Collection

2015-2020

Brittney Melvin

Britta's Book Club edition February 2021
Britta's Book Club can bring authors to your live event.
For more information, to book an event, or permissions for sharing excerpts of this book, please email
brittasbookclub@gmail.com
ISBN: 978-0-578-83894-6
Cover Artwork Ophelia Reclaimed *by Brittney Melvin*
Library of Congress Control Number: 2021900620
Names: Brittney Melvin, 1990- author
Title: Do You Like Butter? : A Poetry Collection / Brittney Melvin
Description: Britta's Book Club paperback edition.
I Massachusetts : Britta's Book Club, 2020

Dedicated in loving memory to my grandfather, Jim Griffin, who used to greet me with, "When are you going to write that book?"

Thank you for believing in me and for teaching me the value of a good story.

Contents

vii	*Introduction*
1	*twenty-something*
21	*psychosomatic*
31	*found poetry & good omens*
45	*the moon makes another cameo*
57	*Do You Like Butter?*
73	*Brooklyn & saying goodbye to Jim*
100	*there will always be dancing*
114	*better than any before*
126	*it's important to feel alive*

Introduction

When I began writing these poems, I was twenty-four years old and going through a personal evolution.

I had just left a life that was wrong for me, and that one brave decision split open my universe and lit my imagination on fire.

While I had been writing since I was a little girl, the medium took on a whole new purpose. It became my lifeline. I wrote my way through everything I encountered, and as a result, these poems were born.

The problem with poetry is that it can feel *too personal*. Even when it's embellishing & augmenting events. Even when the poet is taking literary liberties for a story's sake.

For this reason, it took me a long time to create this collection. In so many ways, I felt past these poems, content to put them at rest with my twenties and the wild abandon of youth. But another part of me knew better.

The process of writing these poems was the deepest form of catharsis. The creation of them brought me peace and clarity. They also brought me to a place of honest self-awareness.

These poems catalogue five years of me wearing my heart on my sleeve, diving into the unknown with a blindfold on, and feeling every feeling like it was my full-time job. And while these poems are raw, vulnerable, and sometimes, a little embarrassing, those characteristics are also what makes them meaningful to me.

These poems, these words – they are as much a part of me as the blood running through my veins, and I'm grateful for all the good things that followed in their wake.

twenty-something

The year Lana Del Rey became religion, lipstick its bible, my Chevy Malibu a sanctuary full of sunset light and sadness. The year I counted selves in lunar phases: whole, half, crescent, the altogether absence of. The year I kept soaring back like Halley's comet, kissing night sky as having suffered through seven and a half decades of separation. Burning up all kinds of wrong atmospheres, letting unknown universes swallow slices of light. Biting into cirrus clouds for breakfast. Tenaciously taking coffee without cream but getting sick of the bitter. Pouring out the bad cup. The year I accepted the dark stuff but decided not to drink it. The year I put the sun in my toothpaste. The year I said, "I can have the whole world, and I will."

— *2015*

Jellyfish

i was fourteen, wading in the Gulf of Mexico with my
cousins, when my uncle found a half-dead jellyfish floating
in the deep end, inspected it in a frisbee, and mistakenly
set it free too close to shore. its lifeless body brushed against
my forearm as it floated by. it was too dead to cling like
they usually do so nobody believed it had actually stung me
until tiny red dots started popping up like chickenpox.
the first time you kissed me i was wearing my seat belt.
you bit my lip so hard that i bled, but i was trying
to forget the taste of a different tongue so i ignored
the injury. your voice got soft for me and i saw
something gentle in you, like the dying jellyfish.

how could something so soft end up wounding me the worst?
so i saw you again two days later, put a pocket knife in your
hands, and told you to carve me into a tally after midnight.
the day of the jellyfish, my mother used sand from our yard
to rub the poison out, and i was back soaking up the
Floridian sunshine the very next day. months later, a
friend laughed at my narrative, saying she had spent
seven days writhing in pain at the Pensacola hospital after
a Man of War wrapped itself around her leg and sent her
into a fever ridden shock. I knew then how thankful I
should be, but I still tell my survival story up North where
nobody has seen a jellyfish for themselves. you floated beside
me for half a second, barely brushing my body, never clinging
to it, and all it took was a little sand and time for the small
crimson bumps to disappear completely. i guess it was
a good thing, but i'm still curious why i collected you in the
frisbee, put a poisonous thing in the water, let it swim
so close to my heart, even if it was half-dead to begin with.

you with your
night sky soul,
dark as the beginning of
the world,
me with my
collection of moonlit kisses
speaking soft commands
as if i could create
celestial prism out of
terrestrial dirt.

— *night sky soul*

The night sky was achingly thirsty for some rain, but the clouds continuously rolled past the moon in a steady, slow-paced movement, as if they were on their way to someplace better. As if they had other parades they planned to rain on.

The lovers sat side by side on a rusty bench on the corner of Main Street. It was the first time he ever held her hand. Really held it. Not in the afterglow of sex, not in the quick clasp to playfully pull her body elsewhere. He didn't wince as she slowly began to make circles on his thumb with hers. She was acutely aware of the way his palm pressed ever so slightly against her own, never quite coming to a firm grasp. She didn't breathe or blink lest the slightest movement stir him into reality and out of her fingers.

They stared at the clouds together, the dark ominous entities that chose to keep moving on, at least for tonight. Maybe tomorrow the storm would come. She didn't mind anymore. With him, she was perfectly content to wade through the loose star particles between heaven and hell, straddling the line between stranger and soulmate.

— *the sweet intoxication of the in between.*

Your fingers fell in love hardest with
things they couldn't take home.

They tried & shook & failed.

In some other universe,
your body is buzzing without the alcohol.

In some other universe,
you are nothing but a breeze dancing
through a set of willow trees.

Ten seconds in the timeframe,
and it's all you ever need.

— *When your bones become a whistle the wind makes.*

There were good things about them, she knew.

There were moments when he'd let her in, soften his voice,

let angels pour out his
trembling mouth, but

she remembered all the bad things, too.

all the women in between these sacred meetings,
the darkest corners filled with monsters he'd
never let her meet,

the way it felt with her head in his lap— wrong,
like a little girl eating lunch in a bathroom stall,
a part of something— but also part of nothing at all.

— *disaster piece*

I don't envy the other girls.
They'll come, they'll go.

I envy your last cigarette.
You trusted its poison in your lungs,
and you let out its smoke knowing
you will never not want more.

– *smoke*

I pray she won't have your eyes. Beautiful and dark like a haunted wood. Full of ghosts. Saturated with secrets I'm scared to decipher. She'll keep the windows open all winter long, because she has got your blood, and it's hot and heavy and restless in her skin.

I can already hear her footsteps falling like rain across my roof because, like you, when the voices inside her get loud, she mutes them by getting high. I can already smell her sadness in the kitchen tiles. Whiskey, cigarette smoke, and cologne I don't recognize.

Your tone lives inside her voice. The excuses are tied to her tongue like they were born there. My stomach will churn every time, like it can still remember the lies growing inside it as she did.

But it's the things that make her just like me which will put her on an edge to be pushed from.

Her love of wild bees– her attachment to anything that can sting while it brings her sweetness.

The way she'll throw her big heart into the ocean, and say,

"*See.*

See, I told you this love could fill the whole thing up."

— *if I ever have a daughter*

She spent so many sleepless nights picking out the pine needles he'd stick in her skin. When she thought she'd finally found them all, more and more would resurface, like delicate little demons waiting to deliver their poisonous punch.

I always warned her to stay away from his forest. I said, "Whenever you finally forget about his ghost, you traipse triumphantly across that burial ground, challenging the sleeping spirits."

She never listened to me. She'd ritualistically run into the thicket as if it was the only place with good oxygen. She'd tangle herself in the brush, buying more time inside his wonderland, shrinking and growing with whatever it was he fed her.

Always withering away altogether whenever it suited him to languidly leave her with no sustenance at all.

— *Stop Stirring up the Spirits*

Text me when you're drunk tomorrow.

Text me when you've had three whiskey sours,
two beers, and ten cigarettes.

Text me when you're drunk and
you don't know your left arm from your right
but you wonder what it would be like to have
my crimson lipstick all over your mouth again.

Text me because you're bored,
because you're curious,
because you want the scent of my perfume
stuck on your t-shirt one last time.

Text me for the hell of it,
because you want my sun soft fingers
bending beneath your bones,
because you still remember how pretty
i look in parking lot light.

Text me because one day we won't be able
to blame our youth or the alcohol.
Because one day I'll have a husband,
a new number, or an apartment in New York City,

and we both know that once that day comes
there will be more than a nine character message
keeping me from crawling back into your bed
to say my goodbye.

— *Just Drunk Text Me.*

Everywhere you go,
men tell you that you're beautiful,
women say they want to set you up with their single sons.
With every claim of adoration, you're still thinking about him.

You tell me he made you feel something.
We both know that asshole never made
you feel anything
but confused.

Remember when he looked blankly at you
from across the parking lot that last time,
as his wasted friend yanked at your hair
and tried to grab at your waist?

He had that white stick perched between his lips,
that steady soulless stare,

I don't want you. You mean nothing. I don't care.

Thirty minutes before that he had his tongue down
your throat and his fingers tangled in your waist-length tresses.

You make excuses in your head as to why he is the way he is.

You don't even really know him.

You've fallen for a concept not an actual person.

Remember that the next time your pretty fingers
try to figure out his phone number.
Put his memory away.

I know you like to chase your vodka with his ghost,
but there's nothing there but a floating white sheet
and a creaking front door.

— *Dear drunk me, you don't even like him when you're sober.*

I will probably be married
someday to someone, somewhere.
I don't really want to be, but
maybe someone, somewhere will change my mind.

Part of me is terrified of being tied down.
That is why I wanted you and all your holes;
Your insatiable lust for freedom
pretty perfectly matched my own.

I'll probably be married one day,
and you won't even know, you won't
even care. I'll have a baby on my hip,
cheerios stuck in my tangled hair.

Will you even recognize me?
Will you even remember I exist?

Probably not.

What am I even saying?
One day I'll be married with a dog,
three cats, burned pot roast–
losing my mind, losing my time.

But maybe the faceless man,
the one I have or haven't met,
will play with my hair, smile at the crumbs,
comb his fingers through like you never do.

Maybe he'll buy me a bouquet of flowers
or just pick some dandelions from
the yard, wipe the Kool Aid stain off my cheek,

draw circles on my arm, bestow kisses cloaked in smiles,
sporadic laughter spilling all over the kitchen tiles.

Maybe, maybe this daydream isn't so dismal.
Maybe, maybe we fear what could make us happy,
because we're grasping onto unhappy fragments,
still holding out hope they'll turn into a complete sentence.

I'll probably be married one day, but
now that I have had time to think,

I could probably get used
to a vase of dandelions
sitting by the kitchen sink.

— *Dandelions*

He told her in hushed tones, stroking her hair through his dirt caked fingertips, "you're the type of woman I would marry, but I'm never going to settle down."

She threw his words into her wine glass, swishing the contents before finally swallowing the poisonous mix. All the while convincing herself that in some other universe somewhere, he'd be mowing the front yard, and she'd be making a bed he'd always come home to.

Do You Like Butter?

It's 3 am and there you are again:
just a blue light buzzing
against my bureau,
just a burning in my bones.
My toes wiggle on the second "bzZz",
as I wonder once again
where you are, what you want.

My sleepless body softly slips out of bed,
And I think, "I should stay."
But I don't.
One five-minute drive later and
I am sitting up, sober, at our spot
in the sand beside the swings.

You lay horizontally, high,
five feet away physically but
five thousand miles from me mentally.

I ache to run my fingers
through that speckled mix
of gray and blackest brown,
but you're so fragile like this.

If I speak you might shatter.
If I move, you might die.
So, I stare at my hands.

I stare at the sky. I
make circles in the sand.

The sand feels sorry for me.
The sky wonders why a girl like
me is so in love with a boy like you.

I wonder, too, until your
lovely limbs shift into silent movement,
as if hearing my holy wish,

crawling inch by tiresome inch
towards my trembling entity.
Your heavy head makes
home of my lap.

I have known you so many times,
but I never know enough to let you
go for good.

As my fingers brush
against salt and pepper
crew cut, I tell myself it's time to say goodbye.

When I finally leave you, like
a summer storm just passing by,

I make sure to spin myself
the stupidest of lies:

that you will never wholly belong
to any world existing
beyond my thighs.

— *things i'll never tell you in poems you'll never read.*

I kissed you
my skin drenched in
parking lot
spotlight

As we kissed,
I envisioned that the earth shook,
and she spoke
through scattered thunder of
the lives I had lived,
spinning stories
I had since forgotten
out of heat lightning and summer breeze

misplaced rhymes that had
haunted me solely in sleep.

I knew again the way the world
could turn within me, I knew that as
the ground opened and trees burned
novelty
could restore
history,
and islands
could be safe houses and not just large lonely sects of
grassy land.

I kissed you
and I knew so much more
than I had before. I kissed you
and all you knew was that
your phone was dying,
my lips tasted like pinot noir,
and I wouldn't be going
home with you
even though I'd been
in your bed
before.

— *Eve never wins for knowing anything*

she had tigers
roaring through her veins,
inhabiting her heart.

when famine finally came,
they fed on her flesh.

they tirelessly tore apart her body
limb for lanky limb.

they sucked sweet liquor
from her sensitive soul,
intoxicated to eat away at her existence.

everyday her eyes
drifted to the firmament
praying please
for manna,

but wild things pray wrong.

wild things wish for a way
to survive without killing
their favorite demons.

— *Wild Things*

She stares at me through slit eyes
like I am all ticking time bomb.
Like I am a fire in the stove and
what if I burn down the kitchen,
or even the whole house?

She marks my movement when
I've had three glasses of wine,
and nostalgia glorifies the past
as the liquor burns my belly.

She knows I want to exalt the
existence of you. She knows
I have always held a knack
for unearthing holiness in
secular fragments.

You and I are an ant hill, an ant hill,
but I have made a mountain
of us in my chest.

My sister cries out, "it's way too high,
please climb down"
donning a sorrowful maternal type frown.

gazing below,
I ascertain aquatic blue replacing solid ground

(i think, "i knew how to swim once")

She winces as I willingly jump in.
Submerging myself in salted sea.
Waves trickling 'cross wounded skin,

"The salt stings but it also heals."

— *I still know how to swim.*

A good muse is an apathetic one.
They won't call you the next day,
so, you read between the lines,
build a pandora's box of the longing.

Open it when you want to feel
the weight of what doesn't love you

Bathe in the chaos of its contents
on Wednesdays when
the weekend nights of forgetting are
distant wishing wells.

You could nurse this torch for two centuries

and still,

there will be no buzz,
just scorched lips,

and an ache that swallows your too big heart,
the way the whale ate Jonah.

psychosomatic

i almost showed up that night.

what a mess that would have been:
me in my party dress,
you with her love all over your fingers.

the police couldn't book you because
there was no blood to be found.
this is because
when you shoot
there is no exit wound.

this is because
the metal is still stuck down deep
like a quarter in the toilet,
like hair in the shower drain
six months since i last snaked it.

and yet you still
go out with that gun,
holding hearts hostage
only to
flush the
fragile organs
down the toilet
with the quarter.

if you're going to be in love,
i wish you'd be good to her.

you were always going to be bad for me,

but

i still hoped that someday you'd find
a way to be good for somebody else.

— *snaking the drain.*

I can tell this man is the kind
who wants his women smitten,
wants them all bloody-knuckled,
wringing their hands in violent
divine supplication – aching, hoping
he will be the everything they can
not be for themselves,

but I am already my own everything.

Which is a problem for men
like him who want to be
worshipped like the God they're
not sure they believe in
when they are
usually sure of
everything.

and you (you thought
you escaped this one)
presented yourself as
a philophobe,
afraid of love,
terrified of
the soft in me,
the way your toes
curled when I kissed your
bristled neck.

but now that love has landed
on your restless shoulder,
like a butterfly,

i
press my trembling
fingers to the wall
in a sort of sad understanding:

i could have wrapped you
in my cocoon, pressed all
my warmest parts against
you for centuries long, but still
nothing would have changed.

you would have always found
your metamorphosis
buried inside

some other girl's touch.

— *it's just science.*

Somebody has forgotten you.

So, you stain your teeth with wild berries,
braid your hair so tightly that the
follicles feel like a razor to the scalp.

This pain has always been psychosomatic.

If you could wash the cut out
with warm water you would

Not. Try, but you'll never get this
country out of your skin.

Those absent r's are a language
you took a bath in but
never rinsed off.

A year from now, this whole situation
will be a four letter word cradled

on the silver spoon called your tongue:

it's not,
it won't be,
it never was
love.

— *Hindsight Bias lets The Past down easy.*

Imagine the worst-case scenario:

He's going to marry her.
He's in love for real this time,
and there's nobody else in his bed.
No other number in his phone.

He's going to marry her, and
he daydreams about the light
in her eyes. The way she loops
her little arms around his middle, laughs
sweetly as she kisses his inner thigh.
This time he is totally unafraid
of all this messy affection
dripping down his throat,
causing an oil spill
in his heart.

He's going to marry her, and
once you hear the news it's
going to hurt like hell.

You'll cause an accident or a scene.
Cry in a crowded supermarket.
Crash into a post office.
Buy a book of stamps and send
him sappy letters addressed to the sea.

Write poems about the world ending.
Buy a cabin in Vermont on a Lake.
Stare at the lake all day. Dream of
drowning yourself in it.

But,
imagine the best case scenario:
he's going to marry her.

You're never going to be alone with him
again. On a street corner. In his truck.

You're never going to feel his eyes
like a machete slicing your mind
into tiny little pieces. Because
he didn't love you, but he got
high off how easily you broke
apart in his hands.

He's going to marry her, so you
will never have to hear him bring
up your first date like a sacred holiday.
Like a day destiny aligned the stars
in his favor. Have him kiss you and
whisper your nickname like it's
a magic word, only to ignore your
messages the next day.

He's going to marry her, and you'll
never have to guess how things
could have been if he was different.
Committed. Kinder. The type to
text you back.

Because he has already
been all those things
for somebody else.

He's going to marry her, but it's not the
tragedy you calculated it to be.

He's going to marry her, but that's just
a way of saying you've got one less
demon to deal with.

He's going to marry her, but that's just
another way of saying,
you are safe,
you are safe,
you are safe.

— *He's going to marry her.*

there was something about
those city bus hands,

dirty but going somewhere,

the constant
miscommunication of signals,

keeping you like
favorite winter coat buried at
the back of my wardrobe,

mistaking you as a
sort of familiar thing
i could return to

when limbs wanted
bone deep warmth.

— *a study on falling in love with public transportation*

Holding your hand
was like running through rain
with a live wire in my pocket.

As risky as it was,
I never felt as alive as I did
almost dying of electrocution.

All you had to do was *ask*, and I would
have said, *yes*. Your voice when
you soften it sounds just like the
hymns my mother used to hum
back when I was small and sad
and trying my best to find
heaven in the harmonies.

Some stranger tried to touch me
last Saturday night. I didn't like him which
is partly why I pushed away his premature kiss, but

even when I meet a man I'm drawn to, I always create a chasm.

I'm not blaming you, but you are the reason why I scare
so easily. Think about it. If you hit a kitten with a car,

she will always set off at the sight of headlights.

— *If you want to know why.*

it was only a palm resting
across your jawbone, the top
of that middle fingertip
grazing your hot
earlobe,

but

love doesn't exist here anymore.
it doesn't feed the children or
put rainwater in the well.

she goes to sleep with a lighter
pressed between her index finger
and thumb. it's not a gun,

but

don't think it's not a sign of danger.
in all her dreams,
the fields are on fire.

and the fields are your hands,
and the fire is her tongue.

— *Night Terrors*

found poetry & good omens

FOUND POETRY AT THE BAR PT. 1

what
is
woman

blue
moon

tiny
tongue
night
whisper
absolute
buzz

FOUND POETRY AT THE BAR PT. 2

worship
woman

as
if
she

the
light
after
night

I'm not in love with you anymore.

But it's been three years since I met you
and still

there has been nobody else.

(I mean,
there have been several somebodies,
but not one like you–
crawling up and out
of my skin,
moving body like the moon
moves water after midnight.)

I did love you.
Not even my own
tongue wants to
admit this, but

there are just some
lyrics limbs will not forget.

— *Muscle Memory*

Never put on your favorite dress out of revenge. That's just a waste. Put it on because it hugs you just right. Ten years from now, you won't even remember the name of the person who didn't text you back or brought another girl to the party, but you will always remember the way it felt to be young, dancing with a good group of friends, laughing just because you're alive.

Never amend your taste or worldview to satisfy the taste or worldview of another person.

Continue to be an open individual. Exchange kind words, listen to people's stories, seek new adventures. There are so many beautiful worlds existing beyond your own. Explore them.

This is a love letter:
this is from me to you, whoever you are.
this is me telling you that it is okay to feel what you're feeling as you feel it.

you are human. to feel is to be human.

if someone has hurt you and you find yourself crying over it,
that doesn't make you weak. that doesn't make you pathetic.
to love a person who can't love you back doesn't make your love bad,

and to stop loving someone doesn't make you a bad person.

you will fall in and out of love,
just as others will fall in and out of love with you.

life keeps moving.
life keeps getting better then worse.
before you know it, you're back to better.

every experience is going to make you
more yourself than you were before.

don't stop loving like your heart is a blank canvas.
don't stop letting other people paint pictures in their favorite colors.
there will be days when you will bleakly stare at the black streaks some used to cover over your favorite parts.

you'll think, this looks so ugly.
you'll think, these stains will stick forever.
but one day they will get painted over by a brighter color,
or, better yet, someone will turn the streak into a building,
or a fortress, or a floating bird against billowy clouds.
you got this. life evolves.

the evolving is what will satisfy you the most.

— wash off your brushes, the world is waiting to marvel at your masterpiece

I guess this is how it happens:
you wake up humming three days in a row,

you smile when you brush your teeth,
stop looking around wishfully at red lights.

you smile at the chipping nail polish,
soaking up the entropy like a good omen,
accepting endings as rebirth, an excuse to
change your favorite color.

the clock doesn't tick like a bomb anymore.

you dance around emphatically to your favorite song.

your coworkers roll their eyes,
but they feel it, too.
everyone feels it,
and everyone
loves it.

you are laughing at silly jokes again,
even the really bad ones you make
yourself.

you put on your highest heels,
apply your brightest lipstick,
declare to the moon, the earth,
the cracks on your bedroom
ceiling:

"I am, I am, I am."

— I am, I am, I am.
after Sylvia Plath's The Bell Jar

in all her dreams she was a tiger,
and when she traipsed through the snake infested thicket

it was poetry.

when she made home of the river flooded rain forest,

nobody said she was strange for sleeping outside.

— IN ALL HER DREAMS SHE WAS A TIGER

what if the whole world walked you to the front door,
painted the sky with your morning laugh,

counted the colors in your eyes and
sang praise to the way your cheeks
flush under firelight?

what if the music lived in your sighs
instead of the thighs of the lover
whose hands don't know
how to touch you like

the grass on the first
day of spring?

— *the whole universe makes you its muse*

THE ACCIDENT

I wonder if I was supposed to die
the day my windshield wiper
stopped working.

I can still smell the peppermint gum
from the police officer's backseat.
Can still see his salt 'n' pepper hair
sopping wet from the hail.

He said something like,
cars can be replaced, but
people's lives are priceless.

When I tried to exit the paddy wagon,
it was locked from the outside in.

I don't believe in love anymore, but
I still believe in friendship.

That is usually enough for me.
Even on the nights when I am being
the worst. Even on the nights I am
too tired to clean off the rain.

NEW FAITH IN OLD BELIEFS

I said,

I don't believe in love anymore.

But that's what the atheists say about God, and

the teenagers say about Santa, and

the mentally ill say about medicine,

so, between believing in
nothing or something,
I'll always choose the latter,

pray as I place cookies on the counter,
take every last pill my doctor prescribes.

Because I want to be brave enough
if the magic isn't out there and
ready for it if it really is.

I wonder if all my favorite poets were also writing about small love,
or if their experiences were something grand.

I was the girl with curiosity coursing through her veins,
and you were the boy with apathy in your blood.

My heart was a rock in the garden.

You were never brave enough to look underneath,
and now I will never know what was there.

— *Unmapped*

The moon:

He swallows
so many
stars
until he collects
enough light
to be whole
once more.

When he is finally full, I
reach across the dark
night sky,

smiling, brushing my
hand against the glow of
galaxies known to us alone:

"You, too?"

– *The Moon and I will always be full again.*

I am sorry that your jaw still aches as if somebody has punched you. But nobody has punched you. So, stop. Stop punishing people that had nothing to do with the fistfight. Or the massacre. Or the demons dancing around your head. Wasn't it you who gave your heart to the guillotine? Begged it to crush the cardiovascular creature till blood poured out like grape juice? Urged onlookers to drink themselves into oblivious fog, only to curse everyone who could not recall your name the next morning?

— tequila will always tell a false version of this story.

the moon makes another cameo

You think of me, and you think of
lipstick stained coffee cups,
perfume soaked syllables,
the question to your least
favorite answer.

You think of me, and you think of
wilting flowers on the windowsill,
my hair always perfect, and my heart
ready to be broken.

You think of touching my
porcelain skin, and you hear plates
crashing in the distance,
every mountain crumbling all
because you said goodbye.

But I am not that delicate.
I am not that dedicated.

I am so good at going,
the doors are jealous.

They can be open, closed, or locked,
but they can never leave.

– *doors*

You kissed me
once you noticed
the blue.

drew
away
disappointed,

even though
it was
so
good.

went home and marked it
on your kitchen calendar

as the day you discovered
not all sad girls taste
like ocean.

— *wading*

history is the dirtiest of all
seven letter words. it means:
"not a part of the present,
going nowhere in the future."

but there you are again,

cheeks & lips flushed with familiar danger.
playing another round of Russian roulette
with your pulmonary veins.

yes, he's looking. no, you're not crazy.
those eyes, a magnet,
your body the refrigerator.

you think it's something special. i'm sorry,
but it's not.

he looks at you like sunlight
through a magnifying glass,
but don't let him burn off your skin.

your entire forest is in flames, and
he is down the street with her cool
hand in his boxers, two glasses of water
on the night stand.

the AC buzzing on full blast.

you think the firetrucks will stir him?
silly girl, with all that noise?

the sirens will scream,
and scream and scream and his heart
won't even skip a beat.

— *the h word*

A Letter to the Moon Written in April

Dear M,

everybody is going out, making
all kinds of messes
underneath your
yellow light—

ten kittens missing, do you think
it's coyotes?

I don't know how to fit into anything anymore
so I stare at my house keys and wonder
how they do it.

At the club, I close my eyes and
move like a country that's
forgetting her anthem.

Another shot and the
walk to the bathroom
feels like it might be
the last time I put
one foot in front
of the other.

Is it true what they say about China?

If I dig a deep enough hole,
will I eventually end up elsewhere?

This is healing. You hurt so bad you don't know how to breathe anymore. You stay in bed when you can, daydream about driving your car into a ditch or off a bridge. You cry a lot, craving to slip out of your skin like a snake shedding its old carcass. You don't want this body anymore. The one with the bad heart and the shaky knees. You drink too much vodka and spend all your Sunday mornings praying into a porcelain toilet bowl, bruising the corner of your palm until it looks like a black and blue tattoo.

Then, like an ice cap just beginning to melt, the earth you stand on shifts ever so gently.

You smile more at strangers. You only sleep with your softest dreams.

When "Hello" comes on the radio, you find yourself telling Adele to kindly fuck off. Because time does heal you, and memories fade further away every day.

Because when the worlds turned inside you, your body became a star. The things that have caused you heartache live in another galaxy now. You have become entirely out of reach: too bright, too changed, too far.

— Healing is like waiting for water to boil. It happens once you step away from the stove.

Somebody new,

I think of you, and I know it could be something. But
everything can be something
if you give it enough water.

if you place the plant in the right window,
it will most certainly get drunk off direct sunlight.

I went to the graveyard today.

I lifted my hands to those cloudless skies and said,
"my favorite ghosts, do you still live here?"

but when I caressed my hands against the cool wet dirt
I found holes where there used to be
skeletons.

I wanted bones but all I found was hollow.

— *RIP*

you say, “i know girls like you”
as you sip your gin,
smoke your bowl,
kiss the crimson off my lips,
those handsome hands trying to
take home my curves
like Saturday night souvenirs.

but you don’t know a damn thing about me.

i am all crystal ball, colored smoke,
curious myth. spooky sensation in my look.
mouth full of magic words,
half fable, half history book.

i am decades deep of studying
strange subtle shifts,
getting you perpetually drunk on the not knowing.

i am the girl
who will give you goosebumps
when you hear my name
in the grocery store,
causing you to spend ages
searching for answers
to the questions in my kiss.

you will turn over every couch cushion
hoping to find an earring, a lipstick,
an excuse to call me later,

and i will be letting all my colors bleed
into the sun, creating prism out of ethereal veins,
turning into a poem while walking away.

— *you’ll be studying me like literature*

I always worry about you. When the sunset light showers into my car windows, I always think, "I hope you're okay." I don't have any reason, any rhyme. I want the moon to fill you up with yellow light. I want you to be happy, really happy, not from some temporal thing, but from some kind of deep peace that comes from a place inside of you. I would pray for you if I prayed anymore. I don't want you to be sad, your sadness kills me the most.

Brittney Melvin

you were fifteen when your father took his
fist to your face and hissed, "you will always be nothing."

i met you nine summers later, and you were still trying to
wash the soap out of your eyes,
the black and blue out of your veins.

i wasn't made to love men like you,
men who taste like cigarettes.
men who kiss you one minute
just to forget your name the next.

despite all that, we were really something
on those sweltering July nights,
laughing in lyrical synchronicity as if
singing hymns to the holy night sky.

i'm no longer mad at the moon for
coloring you my favorite shade of yellow.

all that softness on your skin brought me
the most sacred satisfaction.
even if it was just a trick of light,
even if it was just the glow of grand illusion.

whenever i put on my lipstick, i rarely think
of you kissing the red off. i put on my perfume,
seldom musing over how much you seemed to like it.

on Thursdays i go to the grocery store, and i smile at the
handsome strangers who send me shy hellos in
the cereal aisle. on Saturdays, i flirt with fire in
my teeth, chasing cosmos and kamikaze shots
with foreign tongues who taste nothing like you.

on Monday mornings, i tell my coworkers
of all the new men i meet and the poetry I've penned with
their names now making homes in my margins.

still,
when those words your father
sold you ten summers ago
wake you up

gnashing their teeth and threatening
to swallow you whole,

and you find yourself sulking
in some dark corner cloaked in 3 AM apprehension,

afraid to be awake, afraid to figure out if
your existence ever meant a thing,

i hope you
look out your open window.

i hope you
let the moonlight
fill you up the way it did the nights i thought
i might have loved you,

let that light love you a way mine never could,

let its softness serve as a reminder
from both the universe and me:

you were never nothing,
and you never will be.

— *you were never nothing*

Don't romanticize that night. Or that night. Or that night. Spend new nights combing the stardust out of someone else's tresses. Better yet, drive to Canada. Watch the Aurora Borealis by yourself. Be that brave.

— *Cross the Northern Lights off your bucket list*

Do You Like Butter?

a century has passed since i last opened the curtains. a tribe of dust bunnies crawl off the windowsill as i cast the heavy yellowed cotton aside.

tiny prismatic angels press their palms against my pasty skin, lending their healing light, replacing the sallow gray with an iridescent gold.

my heart opens its mouth and up grows a garden full of dreams dressed as wildflowers. i put together poems out of the prettiest petals. i collect the words into a crown. the sky dons a solid blue gown. every atom of the universe transforms into language. every syllable is sung not spoken.

— *AN AUBADE TO 2016*

you didn't think you could be
this happy, but it's happening.

your mind is a kaleidoscope
full of so many colors
you can't identify
them all.

you can't breathe in all this beautiful
at once, but damn it, if you don't try.

you used
to need
a plane
or a pill
or a lover
to feel this alive,

but now you know
all you need is yourself.

— *lighter days*

think of a space that is open and full of light. it is a place of protection and honesty. a place where you put your love in the ground, and it grows and grows until you are blinded by a forest of evergreens. there are castles you will never hold in your hands, not even in a photograph, but you have got the garden and the river. you will always have flowers to weave and water to drink. you will always have safety in your fingers if you tell them what to do. let this peace rest in your palm. ask it, gently, to stay, and it will.

— *Within*

Brittney Melvin

i say "i am not afraid of anything"
as i run through hell licking gasoline lips,
stroking fingers through foreign follicles, and
drudging up decaying bones, curious to see if
their edges are still sharp enough
to slice straight through me.

but i am afraid.

i am afraid of all the times i've put your name
in my mouth,

swished the nectar soaked syllables
around my gums

using my teeth and tongue to turn the tart liquid
into viscous honey.

i am afraid of how
my entire being aches to explore
every inch of that unknown
promised land
i call your
body.

i am afraid of
all the looks you steal,
the way you save those punchlines
like pennies in your pockets, just
waiting to throw them in my
wishing well as I walk by.

love sounds so sweet when you
attach it to her and you
and that life you've built
with the perfect lawn.

i know better than to cross that line,

i know better than to think that
"love" would be the four letter word
assigned to us if we ever let it get that far.

if we ever let it feel more real
than that marble mouthed goodbye.

if i ever let myself taste that name
for more than ten seconds.

if i ever let myself listen to

every unimaginable thing spoken
between our eyes.

— *A Study on Becoming a Honey Bee*

Someplace there is a person you haven't met yet, and this person has a mouth as bright as the fullest moon. When you kiss, past lives and foreign languages flash across your mind like a secret code you've just unlocked. All at once, you are dying and being born again on lips that look like lips but taste like stardust. The heartaches and the salt come together like cake batter in a mixing bowl. For so long, you begged for something brighter. Something spellbinding and surreal. Even as you prayed on those broken knees, crimson blood dripping through your favorite jeans, you never believed that better days existed. That winter had an ending. That your fingers could be anything but numb.

— *Harrison was Right: Here Comes the Sun*

i can't count how many times i have done something, put myself out there, waved my heart at the universe like a white flag, only to get a result i didn't expect. i am learning to appreciate what i cannot control.

i am proud of every chance i have taken. every wild berry i've consumed without first testing its toxicity. every beautiful place i've ever been has only been reached because i sought something with a wild curiosity and hands unafraid to dig.

— *Waving a white flag at the universe*

When the moon was full last night did your veins turn yellow in its light? I hope so.

I've stopped checking my phone at red lights, looking to see if any of the sad boys I've kissed have come back. They don't matter anymore. You matter. So, I stare at the sky instead, drinking in the blue while I drum my fingers on the steering wheel, wondering what color eyes you have. I wonder what you do at red lights. If you think of the ocean or what you're having for dinner. Do you like this song that I have set to 100? My sister always says I'm going to blow out my speakers. Maybe you have a sister who says the same thing.

When the light turns green, I smile and speed off, as if every forward motion is bringing me a little bit closer to you. I could meet you in 5 hours, 5 months, or 5 years from now. Our hands will touch, and we'll be surprised at the shock, like every set of hands we've felt before were comprised of cardboard. You'll tell me how you've been on so many dates, but no girl has ever made you laugh like this. I'll tell you about all the stoplights I've sat through with the taste of your name on the tip of my tongue.

— *stoplights*

you have lost count of all the times
strangers have told you
you were both
beautiful and sad
all in one breath.

it's nobody's fault, not even your own.
when the earthquake came, the whole world broke.

entire towns split down the middle,
everything precious lost in the cracks.

heartache so big and so wide
not even the Richter scale could calculate
its magnitude,

heartache with no origin but a shaky ground and open palms.

there are houses with lots of windows
and one day,
you'll live in one.

sometimes your bones feel like sandbags and your
head a trophy you no longer have the strength
to carry.

move forward,

press your feet against the pedals,

let that fresh air swallow your sadness.

you've been here before, but you don't
have to stay.

Picture this: me reaching into the night sky and picking a star as if it's a dandelion, making a wish and getting covered in the cosmic dust, smiling each time I see sparkles in the mirror, knowing that everybody i meet is witness to the light of the universe dancing across my skin.

think like this: the ghosts have stopped bathing
in the backyard pool.

you have locked the pantry door.
the demons have forgotten your
kitchen as a feeding place.

write this: a red bicycle parked
within a meadow full of freshly
cut green grass.

your body: a still point. a woven
wreath of wildflowers clinging
to a mass of tangled tresses.

You, free and powerful nymph,
let your laughter live inside
a sky so open it forgets to end.

your ethereal fingertips
press wilted buttercup
beneath tilted chin
while a bright yellow line
dances to the siren
song spilling out
your delicate
throat.

the best thing about this story is
you can always change
the ending to a
happy one.

— *Do You Like Butter?*

i want to tell you that i have changed,
but i never want to speak to you again
so i just write a poem about it.

i got the sudden inclination to purchase
new perfume the other day.

this means i am no longer
leaving my scent behind
in bar rooms where you
might recognize it,
where you might
wonder if i'd
let you put
your hand
between
my legs
one
last
time.

i am no longer traipsing across burial grounds
ghost hunting with cheeks as red as raspberries
plucked on an early May morning.

i don't want anything dead unless
it is flowers,

picked and cut fresh
with kitchen scissors.

"i don't want you anymore,"

i tell myself
and actually
mean it.

— *I want flowers*

do you remember last winter? laying in the dark,
drinking white wine, listening to Lana,

picking red polish off your week-old manicure.

do you remember the first of February?

you climbed that willow tree even when you
you knew that the branches were broken,
smiled as you heard that first snap,
sang a twisted song as you let

your still limbs sink to the bottom of the river?

this is healing. when you look in the mirror,
and you've stopped imagining Ophelia.

there's nothing beautiful about boys who
prefer ghosts over living girls.

there's nothing alluring about a mad man
who wants you all stringy hair and withered flowers,
angry over you asking for a t-shirt, dissatisfied when you say
which side of the bed you slept on last time.

this is healing. when you go out drinking and don't
even play with the concept of conjuring the spirits.

when you no longer want anything to do with anyone
who doesn't look at you without seeing the entire universe
present in the crystal ball called your eyes.

— you're holding a whole lifetime in one look

It wasn't love.
(It was sinking sand.)

Do you know how this story ends?
I dug myself out
the way I always do.

I'm sorry. I know now
that I could never love you
the way I've written about
loving you,

that if you ever invited me to
stay at your station, to create a home
out of your heavy wandering heart,

I would have seated myself
on a new bus the very
next morning,

craving the sort of leather seat
with the cracks.

— *a study on falling in love with public transportation pt. 2*

Brooklyn
&
saying goodbye to Jim

Wait for
the new dreams
to boil
without
watching
the water.

the future has
nothing at all
to do with us.

let us be isolated,
let us be our own entity.
our pasts are not invited
either.

let us take off our shoes,
lose our breath in laughter
as we hastily but steadily
move my old mauve couch.

let us play twister in our socks.
tell me your favorite color
and if you like milk in your coffee.

we don't need to clean up our mess.
tell me that you prefer my perfume
over the scent of pine and lysol
anyway.

— *Let's Just Exist in the Same Room Together*

I want so badly not to be the girl who writes about love. The absence of it, the hope for it. I want so badly to run my fingers through your dark hair and feel nothing but the poetry pulsating through my veins. Everyone asks, “Does he make your stomach flop?” The thing is, I stopped bothering with butterflies long ago. All I crave now is the cool sweat after fever dream. All I crave now is fire singed fingertips.

— *I want so badly*

I am not in love with anyone, and the love still lives. Thriving without host. Evolved past its parasitic state. I am not in love with anyone, and yet, still holy walks through haunted woods. Still shaking hands under crisp clean sheets. I am not in love with anyone, but the poems still come, pressing their tongues against my tongue. Bruising my neck all night long. Begging me not to stop, not to stop.

— *I am not in love with anyone, after Trista Mateer*

If this dissipates, I'll be
Disappointed but more
than alright.

Last night,
I came across a
Big Band playing
outside the
Brooklyn Library–

I thought of
someone I used
to love and how

if he was standing
two feet in front of me,

I would not recognize
him at all.

–*Transitory*

I am amazed by
the science of
how your body
evolved me

transforming every
molecule of

my soul in instant
metamorphosis

and today I saw
your face

and it didn't even
phase me.

– may all your unrequited love stories end in nonchalance.

My Own Version of Auld Lang Syne –

Say my name in
another language
on another planet,

try to make me so soft
I bend beneath your teeth.

Remember now when it worked.

Remind yourself
how weak I was
in your arms, and now,

I can’t even
assign them
an adjective.

Something I have wanted but never gotten:

A man who looks
at me like I
am a firefly

dancing in summer air
to the music

of my own laughter,

who says he will smash
his mason jar into a
million pieces,

who looks at me
all aglow

knowing I am my own sky,
and I belong to myself.

I want it wild and dedicated.

I hate when people say,
"enjoy your freedom while it lasts."

Why can't I be free and in love?

I like to think that when
I meet the right person,
I will lose nothing, that

the right person will look
at me and think,

"She can't be contained,
and I don't want her
limited in any way."

The weather report lied to me,
and I am now sitting underneath
a big blue sky in Prospect Park
watching happy dogs.

– don't believe everything you're told

I never asked you things
I still want to know like
how old were you when
you first learned to fly?

And when you
put on that pilot's hat, did your hands
begin to shake, or did you think only of

the freedom, the air,
all the sky in the palms of your hands?

the world was about to become
both bigger and smaller at exactly the same time.

I could have loved you like that,
a simultaneous disruption of the elements.

My molecules, your molecules, colliding.

A beautiful mark for meteorology.

A sort of Big Bang,
an open unexplainable flame

followed by a long loud rain.

— *A Study of Our Atmospheres if Shared*

I was sad at first,
but then I woke up Dancing.

Did you ever hear the story
of the girl who didn't get
what she wanted?

She placed a Tiger Lily
behind her ear,
walked West,

and found it Somewhere Else.

– the moment I began moving on without looking back

neon dreams –

There were dark days when
all I wanted to be was
someone and somewhere else.

It wasn't until I took my body
to the biggest city I could find
that I found out not even
the glitter of New York

could inspire and illuminate
my world like the light
living inside me.

THE PORTRAIT

I am in a city that I love (perhaps it's
this one, perhaps I have finally found
my sweet spot), and we are
in our kitchen, sometimes sober
sometimes three glasses thick in sticky
sweet wine.

Always laughing
and always dancing

and always being sure of all the little paths
that brought us through the darkest alleys
and distracting detours until we were
standing in the same room together
ignoring chipped paint and smiling.

Go to the city,

then leave it
if you'd like.

Follow the dream
until it's out of your system –

dance in some strange universe
you manifested with your mind,

then abandon the dream
once it no longer serves you.

Find a new dream
or *many* new dreams.

Rake the dreams into a pile
like leaves. Scatter and throw

them up in the air.

Ask the
sky how
it learned
to rain
and snow
and spread its
arms out
wide.

The rhythm buries itself
inside my bones until
a new country
is born.

I was beautiful before
he/they/you told me;

I run down the street
and with every stride–
I am really something.

I was and am
and have
never been,

If I speak/smile/sing/move,
do you think you own me?

Are you angry
when I point
at the shackles
(a thing you wanted wild)
and I start to scream?

I want it Wonderful.
I want it Easy,
like holding somebody's
hand in my sleep.

Like Etta James on repeat.

The Slow Smooth Sound

of something good
knocking on
my door.

I want it all,
I want it right,
and I want it

Every. Single. Day.

— *Dear Universe*

My laughter opens up the sky
as I consider the absolute absurdity of
the drunken Freudian slip, "I love you"
delivered with an unwanted pedestal
I'd never dream to stand on.

Every time I've ever wanted
something bad it was because
I was curious in the way a child will
dangle finger over open flame,

but my skin is always smart enough
to get away before giving anything
the power
to burn
it off.

– when bad boys pretend they love you

I was driving down the highway
and thinking of you fondly
when a rock hit my window

and it was like God himself was saying,
"Wake the fuck up."

Because between
the sunburn, lack of sleep,
and gilded illusions,

it could be easy
to explain away
your bad behavior,

but Heaven still knows
there's no way
you'll ever be
good for me.

– *an autobiography of my morning commute*

To Somebody I Have Never Met,

You are the one
I have always
known about

even the stars
tremble

to find out how
I'll love you.

I don't read my horoscope anymore.

There are some fates we're given
and some fates we choose,

but none of them are written on a wrinkled
piece of magazine paper.

And anyways, wouldn't you rather
stare at the stars instead of
analyzing them?

I want to pour the sky a cup of coffee
and ask it, "where are you taking
me dancing tonight?"

Sometimes there is nothing more
important than not knowing
what comes next.

– date nights with the sky

My favorite notebook
is falling apart
and last night
we went out drinking
which was fine
until the pain came back
like a boomerang
and we sobbed for what
felt like days.

I don’t want to imagine this life
without you, but you
won't have to worry,

The love and the stories
are stored inside
our hearts forever.

Your spirit is a peace we
will always get to keep.

– when my grandfather was dying

Thirty-three years ago
you saw her having dinner
with a friend, and the
whole world changed.

Every other moment after
belonged to the two of you,
and not one day passed
without you talking about
how wonderful it all was.

Today, there is no sun
to distract me so I am
wading through the darkness
thinking of this beautiful
love between the two of you,

how one spring it shot up
like a daisy in the pavement
and turned into the thickest forest
permeating everything in sight.

– Nana and Jim

It wasn't until 9
last night when
the tears finally came,

and I found myself
staring down at my palm
in surprised observation.

The loss of you is so large,
it doesn't hit me.

I just sit inside it
trying to do ordinary things
like driving my car
or writing a poem.

Five minutes ago, I was downstairs,
and I saw your dress shoes
underneath the bathroom sink,

which was the universe
saying something I already know–

there are so many spaces in my life
nobody but you
will ever fill.

I stare at the slice
of Big Blue Sky hanging
above me, wondering
how I can be happy
in a world without you.

All I can think of is
the wonderful way you loved,
the American flag
folded in a triangle,
the way you loved,
all the wilted flowers
bunched together on my bureau,
and –

The way you loved,
The way you loved,
The way you loved.

there will always be dancing

I saw you in a dream before I met you.

I couldn't count the freckles on your cheek,
but I saw your hands:

messy and beautiful like Florida rain
in the summertime.

And your smile was the Best Thing.

You smiled like the sun was inside you,
and while we looked at each other
another sun grew inside my chest, too.

That was when I knew you were real,
because dream phantoms
can't create all that joy.

— *Premonition*

California cast a spell
and I am
stumbling drunk
off its audacity
to build new dreams
into a heart that
thought it might
be done with wandering.

Wouldn't it be something
if this magic never wore off?

If I woke up tomorrow
and this glow just kept growing?

The dancefloor doesn't think
twice, it just brings me
everywhere all at once
like a magic trick
Google does not hold
the answer to.

Even if it did,
I don't want to know
the recipe of this spell,

the secret sauce that
constitutes the elixir.

for the rest of my life,
the mystery of it will
be bringing me this
beautiful rush
of belonging to a
rhythm all
my own.

There is a magic energy
running through
every part of my body,

making me a believer in better things
touching everything
I touch,

lighting every lantern,

delivering every
last dream
safely home.

I have always been
The Something Wonderful
I spent all those silly
years waiting for,
but still –

I would like something light and sweet

for an hour or two
(or maybe as long as I live.)

Something I know
I've never had
but have imagined
so often that
the image is

secured inside my mind
like a memory
just waiting
to sprout.

For a split second
you could've been something
to her,

but now she is
dancing in a dream universe
you'll never get to taste.

when you catch her eye
there is this shared secret

and the laugh in her look is

free from pain
and never

at your expense.

She used to choose her lovers
like teenagers select their booze.

It didn't matter how cheap the quality
as long as it got her drunk good and fast.

Now, she no longer lets bad love in the door.

She lets the good inside her draw good things back.

She dances alone under a red moon, and
it brings her joy instead of sadness.

There is a light behind her eyes, and

she has never before felt so
beautiful and happy and free.

I reclaim joy
like a lost language
like a story my tongue
knew once but forgot
how to tell. My teeth vibrate
with the wonder
of remembered music.

I transform a feeling
into a way of life.

While others walk,
my body will only dance.

There were dark days
when she'd whisper with
shallow breath,

"you did this to yourself"

But tonight,
her body was
totally golden, and
when she whispered those
same words, "i brought this
upon myself"– her soul filled up

with the unmistakable
presence of manifested joy.

You have done the good work.

You have sat cross-legged on the floor
tying knot after knot after knot
til you were surrounded by
smooth edges.

you have planted yourself on good ground.

Your heart tender and ready
but also loud and strong.

Its rhythm is soothing
like precipitation in
a rainforest
lulling a
jungle
to sleep.

Tell me a ghost story,
then show me the
blanket and the scissors
you used for the holes.

Undress your spookiest tales
until we see them all
for what they really are:

a mind trick, a strong wind,
a dark blue bike
left in the shadows.

Flash your light on
the coyotes and the goblins,

then let them and me
and the entire world know

none of it can touch you.

– *Spooky Good*

Today I told the story
of how my grandfather
saved me from drowning.

I still remember
watching the walking stick
in the water, feeling my
small weight sinking
slowly for a minute,

before being brought up
to a sea of concerned faces.

I think of that moment
as a sort of origin story;

how no matter how far
down I go,

I always rise again.

REFLECTION

Walk through your hometown
on an early weekend morning
when everybody else is sleeping.

Find your body taking you down streets
you forgot existed.

Watch the snow melt.
Think of it as a pact between you and the Universe.

Look over the ages lovingly.

Remind yourself of how you are different
and how you are the same.

better than any before

I wanted love
but only if it
lent me more light
than I knew what to do with.

I dreamt it
brave and kind.

I dreamt it right or
not at all.

It is difficult to describe
all the beautiful things happening,
so I will just say this –

What I've got now is better
than any before.

What I've got now is working
away my walls
and replacing
them with sky.

I try again
to write about you,
but my words can't match
what you're doing to my heart.

I don't want it to end, but
even if I walk away with just these
few wonderful days,

you are something so good.

You are the one
from all my someday poems.

I never knew exactly
when it would happen.

I lived thousands of lifetimes
in one body before the Universe
made it so.

The more grateful I grew, Gravity drew us closer.

In every alternate reality, the dream of us
was always there.

— *Will*

Each week of wanting
felt like ages,
but to our angels,
the years passed
like shooting stars.

While I was wondering
when I was going to meet you,
they were patiently
watching the planets
until everything
was perfectly aligned.

Brittney Melvin

Before I met you,
I learned to dance by myself
and love it.

I would walk and walk and walk and
find gratitude for every branch in
every tree, paint pictures with my alone
and call all the shades lavender.

Before you first kissed me,
I lived hundreds of lives in
twenty-eight years, and sometimes,
I entertain the magical idea that
there were even more before that –

That we each lived many lifetimes and
in every one, you would be at the end
of all the pain,

the rainbow after so many strange storms.
That in each life,

right before I would decide
to shutter all my windows

your colors would splash against
my kitchen counter.

And each time, I sigh.

Each time I say, I could have done it by myself,
but I'm glad you showed up.

She awoke one day
with the wonderful idea
to ask the sky to
lend her its open,
and since then,
she has learned
the truth that
every limitation
was actually a
hollow mirage.

She was reborn
out of a realized dream

and from then forward
she found that everything
she ever wanted
was attainable
as long as
she asked.

Remember a time
when you knew nothing
about something
that mattered to you.

Return to that hunger.

Ask it to be present
in everything you do.

– *beginner's mind*

The accident was a turning point.

Ice.
Traffic.
A broken motor vehicle.

If it didn't happen,
my whole life could've
been different.

Today I drove by the street
where it went down and watched two cars
come close to repeating my history.

Tires squealed, but there
was no collision.

In some other universe,
the firetrucks came.

– *parallel*

The year love
landed on your lap, and
it was not an illusion.

The year you made peace treaties
with ghosts
and woke up
unhaunted.

The year you took five flights out
and six flights home.

The year that you got what you wanted
while whispering over and over,

"There is still so
much more
to learn."

– 2018

it’s important to feel alive

Here is a close-up of the lake –
a bird's eye view of
that first feeling
of belonging.

Back when this person you
became was as large and unknown
as the sky above you,

and all you knew was
all you know now:

It's important to feel alive.

I hear one song, and
I am brought back

1997 fresh vegetable stand

the smell of strawberries and
mud pies, planting skittles
waiting for the rainbow, a promise of something

I don't know what
except maybe that the sun would be there
with the bay in the morning,

that the world would
continue to be
what we dreamed
and believed it to be.

I hear one song and so many

other summers appear in my mind

long forgotten lakeside days
emerging like

characters from a television show
I spent seven
years attaching myself to

only to never think
of them again
once the
series
ends.

Call me in a dream when you read this

Call me in a dream when you read this.
We can meet in some remote corner
of our girlhood before
time turned you into unknown stranger –

before we became women with
worlds of experience
glowing beneath our
aging skin like diamonds,
making us rich enough
to live our lives comfortably
without each other.

i
could have sworn
you'd be a staple.

kitchen scissors, paper towels

It turns out you don't always need
the people, places, and things
you thought you did.

It's been
something like 1500 days since
we last spoke

and we're both okay,

but

call me in a dream and I can fill you in on everything.
call me in a dream because
our friendship was born in the idyllic wake
of childhood imagination,

and in that world it will
always find its home.

I wish these words could swallow me up and evolve me into a light thing. I want the openness of past lives without the pain. Let the language wash over my body like the waves of the bay behind my childhood home. Add the moon and my heart and the wind. Subtract everything that isn't pretty or peaceful or sweet. I want the poem to change me until everybody forgets my name and calls me brand new.

In a dream,
you stood
at the top
of a mountain.

Years later, you
arrived at the
same place, except
this time,
it was your reality.

You brought yourself to this imagined wonderland,
and your body was the only vehicle
you used.

Letting bad energy
into this precious
life is like
building a greenhouse

only to grow poisonous fruit.

I refuse to be a carrier pigeon
for any thought
that doesn't serve me.

The only thing stopping me
from living the life I have
imagined is nothing
at all.

The Universe has and always will
give me exactly what I want.

I will keep building on the
best parts until my whole world
is wholly constructed
of realized dreams.

– thoughts from the Hingham Shipyard

You pacify the wild thing inside you,
but don't ever kill it.

Its every molecule
is yours.

With all its chaos,
it also brings you
magic.

Your mind
is a map.

You dictate its direction;

you control all of the coordinates.

Whenever the water gets too high, you still
your world on its axis.

You are the architect of your
geography, and you know
every way home.

ACKNOWLEDGEMENTS

Thank you to my sister, Amanda, who taught me that I needed to learn to love myself. You helped me survive my greatest heartbreaks and most challenging seasons, and your unconditional love continues to bless my life every day.

Thank you to Adam, Jake, Mum, Dad, Nana, Jim, and James Poirier for always believing in me and my art.

Thank you to Brittany Schiedow for constantly sending me videos of you scrolling through all of my poems and pressuring me, out of love, to publish them into a book. You kept me accountable in a way nobody else did.

Thank you, Jenn Luchon, for the clarity, laughter, and soul cleansing friendship.

Monica Broughton, you are and have been such a light in my life during all the years I wrote these poems. I am forever thankful for you.

Thank you to my other friends and family members who kept encouraging me to hone my craft.

Thank you to everyone who picked up this book and read it. It means very much to me that you took the time to read these words.

Finally, thank you to Will, "the one from all my someday poems." The stars used to tremble to find out how we'd love each other, until one day the universe brought us together again. I'm so thankful for you, my kindhearted and wonderful partner. Sharing a life with you is a treasured existence.

ABOUT THE AUTHOR

Brittney Melvin has been writing poetry since she was seven years old.

Besides reading & writing, Brittney enjoys dancing, trips to the mountains, and marveling at the moon. She is deeply grateful for creativity, good people, and the home she shares with her wonderful fiancé Will.

She resides in Massachusetts (where she was born and mostly raised) but has had adventures in Brooklyn & Pensacola, Florida.

You can find her on Instagram @brittney.melvin posting about her work and other artists who inspire her.

Made in the USA
Middletown, DE
01 June 2021

40830263R00090